Sometimes Life

Tiffany Stretch

BookLeaf
Publishing

India | USA | UK

Presentation by *BookLeaf Publishing*

Web: www.bookleafpub.com

E-mail: info@bookleafpub.com

ISBN: 9789358315301

First edition 2023

Alex

My dog named Alex liked to chew
She especially enjoyed my favorite green shoe
Alex is a best friend
She loves until the end
With Alex in stride I have nothing to lose

Lady

Found in the ravine,
Poor puppy was quite a scene!
She cleaned up real nice.
Played, and sang and full of delight.
Cuddly and loyal, unless there's a fright!
Inseparable family now,
What a doggy, dog life!

Pair-a

3

Such a pretty kitten
We called you Paris, Paris Hilton.
Go to the vet,
Surprise present we get!
Pair-a-matching set, I said?
Paris is now Para
You can find him outside prowlin'!

Cry Baby Kitty

The curious kitten
Smelled cucumber melon
"Not too close, the candle is hot!"
Up in flames one whisker shot
Poor baby kitty cried a few tears
Princess rocked that crooked whisker for years!

Look

5

I look not to have the green grass on the other
side,
I look to tend my garden so it is fruitful and
grows toward the grass
You, Grass are consistent while I, Garden am
beauty everchanging.
The garden processes complex emotions and
intertwining thoughts;
The grass moves with graceful strength and
straight honesty.
I look to the barren land between
Grass and Garden tended together
Blended and balanced, one not without the other
Growing becoming a paradise of happiness and
harmony
I look to see what I have to enrich the barren
land
I look to have it all, the grass, the garden and
everything in between.

Yearn

I feel myself open like a flower every time I
think about you.
The sensation wraps tightly around the void,
shortening my breath
Like a wave, enveloping the depth, the root of
me.
Brief hold, releasing my void, I feel the strength
as it lets go and hits the very tip of my soul
Rebounding, reversing and showering my love
upon the very thought of you,
Taking my breath away.
I yearn for you.

The Love I Dream Of

The love I dream of is consistent in action
Vulnerable enough to apologize and admit
wrong
Hardworking enough to provide and repair the
home and matters of the heart
Encompasses awareness to recognize any
growing distance between us
The love I dream of is the center of my universe
Looks at me as brightly as the sun shines
Burns with desire as hot as a solar flare
Caresses me like the warmth that caresses the
earth
The love I dream of is peace and a master of
calm
Taming the tumultuous fears within
Courageous and honest
He opens his heart with words
Gentle and patient
He is my partner in all things
Strength and fortitude
He encourages positive mindset
Secure in his commitment
Secure in my commitment
The love I dream of loves me as I am

Anxiety

Why do I obsess?
Why do I worry?
Everything is hurry, hurry, hurry!
What is everything?
What is so important?
Life is only good if you have a fortune!

Ghost

9

I will disappear
I will not interfere
Leaving is easy
You can't see my tears
You will not see me
You will not know me
I will disappear
You will not interfere

Worth

You said we will never be together
I believed you
even though I did not want that
I appreciate you keeping me at a distance
I stayed focused on myself and my healing
I knew you are not good for me
But, it was when you cut off your connection to
me
I was able to see how bad you really were to me
I was over time able to cut my connection to you
It was difficult and painful and took time
When I made progress you would come
To take back your power
But I am worthy of a love better than this

A Single Memory

Sudden
Longing
Desperate
Hollow
Flooding
Part of my heart floats externally above my
breast
The center of my throat contracts into a round
lump
A passing thought paused just long enough
The final ram cracks the castle barricades
Forcing past the gates
Each tear burns, the piercing prick of betrayal
Remember

Depression

I want to leave
Everything
Everyone
Some days, most days

Grief

There cannot be more pain
All the pain is in me
If I hang on to it
No more will reach me
No more can hurt me
If I never let it go
My heart will have no room for more

Hear

The silence is deafening
My ears constantly ringing
The sunlight is blinding
My eyes quickly tiring
The conversation is muting
My tongue sharply cutting

Numb

15

I want to go out
But where can I go
Knowing I could hurt them more
How can I go out and
Numb the pain and suffering
Without anyone knowing I hurt

Why

Who hurt you so badly you bleed onto
innocents?
You see the blood and try to find their wounds
Unknowing it is you that was wounded long ago
You now hold the knife
Deeply cutting, slowly bleeding out anyone who
gets near

I Need

Meeting my needs does not mean do it alone
Meeting my needs does not mean not asking for
help
Meeting my needs does not mean not accepting
help
A lifetime of unmet needs and wants
A dream of a life I cannot obtain alone
Having needs is not shameful
Having wants is not shameful
I end up here
Unwilling to ask for help
Unwilling to accept offered help
Doing it alone
Unable to identify and communicate needs and
wants
Dreaming of a life fulfilled

Love and Light

Unapologetic and dangerous
Things she has never told anyone
Too dark for whispers, aware
How easily the darkness can consume her
It is not scary, it is home.
There is no pain for her in the darkness, only
others.
She has worked hard to cultivate the light
Into brightness that cannot be dimmed.
She needs the light to survive,
Somehow…now… she thinks she needs the
darkness too

First Love

Oh, my love
You were always there when I needed you
You were always there when I wanted you
You were so much fun and made me smile
You gave me strength and courage

You did not love me
You took away my power
You took away my bravery
You left me ill and unhealthy
You made me think you were helping
You were killing me slowly
Alcohol, my first true love

Presence

Your presence brings strength, allowing me to
soften
Your presence brings companionship, filling the
void of my loneliness
Your presence brings freedom for my heart to
find peace
Your presence brings safety providing a life
without fear

Found

Free from the things that no longer serve her
She is her own worst enemy.
Embrace her, allow her in
Cohesive and complementary
Yin and yang
Warrior and monk
Darkness and light
Her broken, yet eager heart cries out
Restore balance within
Be your truest self without
Happiness in you is service and gratitude